Horses & Heroes

Horses & Heroes

The photography of John Minoprio

SWAN HILL PRESS

First published in the UK in 2000
by Swan Hill Press, an imprint of Airlife Publishing Ltd

British Library Cataloguing-in-Publication Data
A catalogue record for this book
is available from the British Library

ISBN 1 84037 128 5

Printed in Hong Kong

Swan Hill Press

an imprint of Airlife Publishing Ltd
101 Longden Road, Shrewsbury, SY3 9EB, England
E-mail: airlife@airlifebooks.com
Website: www.airlifebooks.com

Dedication

FOR CAROLINE

'No hour of life is lost that is spent in the saddle'

WINSTON S. CHURCHILL
My Early Life – 1930

Preface

This book is about my 40-year love affair with photography and taking pictures of horses. Originally, and in Millennium year, the title *Celebration of the Horse* seemed right. But, thinking it over, the book focuses on people as much as horses. *Horses & Heroes* reflects my admiration for horsemen and women. I have found in them the virtues of courage, grace beyond beauty and, when I prevailed upon them for a picture, a charming accommodation.

Although photography is my hobby, I have taken money on a 'nice work, if you can get it' basis. My first paid assignment was for Jack Wood, Sports Correspondent of the *Daily Mail*. At Wentworth, for the 1956 Canada Cup, he spotted me with a new camera around my neck by the 18th green. He buttonholed me to photograph a 17-year old Swedish golfer, barred by the L.G.U., from playing in the Ladies' Championship wearing 'hot pants'. The picture appeared in the *Daily Mail* under the headline 'Golf in Briefs? Oh No!' My fee was £3.

My interest in photographing horses was encouraged by Lt. Col. C.E.G. Hope of D.J. Murphy Publishers Limited, 19 Charing Cross Road, editor of the monthly magazines *Light Horse* and *Pony*, cover price one shilling and sixpence (7½p).

It was Colonel Hope who made it possible for me to go to the great horse shows – Windsor, Richmond, The White City, and Dublin – as well as Badminton, where I stood under the tree in the ring for the showjumping in those old informal days. Colonel Hope, an Indian Army Cavalry Officer, gave me a start. I shall always remember him and I hope he would have liked this book.

Photography was much simpler in those days. The small Leica, with its collapsible 50mm standard lens, served me well. Later, I acquired a shopful of lenses, cameras and gadgetry, but my photography did not improve.

I began with black and white. Then, in 1972 I switched to colour. I found this very difficult. There was always the wrong colour in the wrong place, spoiling the picture. I envied the artist's freedom of palette.

Ira Gershwin, who wrote the words for his brother's songs, called his autobiography *Lyrics on Several Occasions*. This collection of photographs, snapshots in time, show horses on several occasions, and people, too. For me, they are heroes for the pleasure they have provided – and I thank them all.

JOHN MINOPRIO
Threapwood
2000

Contents

'He makes it look easy' – Sam Marsh

I have a sketch of Sam Marsh by F.A. Stewart. He is jumping a big fence out hunting in perfect style. The caption reads 'he makes it look easy'. But this was the man whom the famous riding master Lt. Col. Jack Hance described as 'the finest all-round horseman this country has seen for 50 years'. Seeing me with my camera, he beckoned ... 'would you like a picture?'

On Mrs. Soanes' Golden Madonna at his local show, Edenbridge and Oxted 1960.

Artist of the Show Ring – Ann Davy

Annie Davy looked sublime. She rode Hugh Haldin's stunning show horses to perfection, an art she learned from that show producer of spell-binding style, Count Robert Orssich. Here she is on two of Mr. Haldin's champions – the hack Free as Air at the Royal International Horse Show, White City, and the hunter Marksman at Kent County Show 1962.

11

Youthful sensation – Jennie Bullen

*The teenage Jennie Bullen on Miss Stubbings' champion hack Desert
Storm, a sensation at The White City in 1962. The black mare, all lightness
and gaiety, went beautifully for its young rider. Together they won many
championships, including the Winston Churchill Cup at the Royal
International Horse Show, awarded on the applause of the crowd.*

Pre-war elegance – Ladies' Hunter Judges

The starched formality of the Ladies' Hunter Class at Windsor in 1962. The immaculate judges, Lady Stanier and the Honourable Lady Hardy, reflect the highest of horse show style. Before them, in the gleaming silk hat and white stock that was de rigeur, is Miss Jane Talbot-Clayton, showing a fine chestnut hunter. This is pre-war elegance and reminds me of Lionel Edwards' painting of the same class at flower-decked Olympia.

Concentration – Judging

Mrs. Nigel Pease judging a Ladies' Hunter Class at Dublin. To judge at Dublin is an honour as well as an arduous task, for the classes are big. Concentration must not wane, even on a hot early August day. Ailsa Pease, a frequent judge at major shows, brought a lifetime's experience of horses to the task. It is often said of horsewomen, 'she looks wonderful in riding clothes' – hinting, perhaps, that she looked less than good in anything else. But, whether showing a horse, judging, or dining out afterwards, Mrs. Pease looked perfect.

Judges

Mrs. Dorian Williams and Mrs. J.B. Ross (the former Miss Ann Davy) can relax having completed their judging of a Small Hunter class at Windsor. It looks as though they are heading for the President's tent and a welcome gin and tonic. I fear this picture looks a candidate for one of those competitions 'What are they saying to each other?' inspired by the cover of Private Eye. 1971.

Champion Pony

Pollyanna, the champion pony at Windsor in 1962. Owned by Mrs. K.V. Coates and Mr. A.S. Deptford, and ridden by Aly Pattinson. This 4 year old chestnut mare by Bwlch Valentino out of Pretty Polly, won many championships. Mrs. Coates and Mr. Deptford were leading show pony breeders and exhibitors in the post-war years, and Pollyanna's dam was champion at Windsor in 1951 and 1952. Aly 'trained on', as they say in racing, to take the Burghley Three Day Event title on Carawich in 1975.

The Martin-Bird Sisters

Angela and Tessa Martin-Bird from Coolham in Sussex, with the marvellously well-matched Arden Dawn and Hurtwood Lucinda, winning the Pair of Children's Ponies 14.2hh Class at Windsor in 1962. The sisters, with their blonde hair, finely tailored jackets, and pink carnations, had won the previous year and were unbeatable. They had a long career in show ponies, but told me they wanted to go eventing. And they did. Both rode at Badminton – Angela on Grey Cloud was runner-up in 1969.

The Royal Welsh Show

Green and tranquil, Builth Wells is the home of the Royal Welsh Show. One feels in the very centre of Wales. It has quiet calm, reflected in the photograph of this young girl with her mare and foal waiting her turn. 1970.

Dublin – The Family Show

LEFT: *Children picnic in the hunter lines at Dublin. This is a show for the family and they come from 'all over'. Dublin horses are for sale and the young keep vigil over their precious charges. This is 1970, when horsey girls still wore headscarves.*

BELOW: *Little appears to have changed – this is the medium weight hunter lines in 1997.*

Dublin Style

Afternoon in Dublin, and a hunter class, with a competitor who is a model of tailored elegance as she waits to present her horse to the judges. 1970.

Leg-up

Judges, with the prospect of a long line of hunters to ride, value a leg-up, assuming there is a competent person to give it. In side-saddle classes, it is essential. Here a show hunter exhibitor gets a welcome lift. Dublin 1970.

The Veterinary Ring

Sheer pleasure beams from a girl's smiling face as she tries a horse in Dublin's Veterinary Ring. The Royal Dublin Society, founded in 1731, staged shows to encourage owners to breed and sell horses, and the Veterinary Ring is where the business is done.

The Kiss

*'In Dublin's fair City, where girls are so pretty,
I first set my eyes on sweet Molly Malone;'*

*Well, perhaps this young man has found his Molly Malone and good luck
to both of them. Dublin 1997.*

The Rosette Winner with the Laughing Face

A gentle guiding hand for this rosette winner, and her laughing face reveals her delight. Showing ponies should be fun and a generation ago, it was. To take part was reward enough. Today, sky-high prices for ponies make winning the name of the game.

24

Portrait of Angela Cooper

A longer than usual lens bridged the distance to make this portrait of Lady Cooper possible. A well-known show rider and judge, the veil and bowler tells that this is a Ladies' Hunter Class. Royal Show 1970.

Touch of Magic – Mark Russell

Lord and Lady Hugh Russell, seeking stud card photographs of their grey Crabbet-bred Arabian stallion, Touch of Magic, suggested their one-year-old son, Mark, appear to illustrate the horse's delightful temperament. Here he is, taking my direction like a pro, as we set up the shot. Bathampton House, Wylye, Wiltshire. 1961.

The Professional

The techno-wizardry of cameras and zoom lenses, and the magazines that 'bench test' them, with daunting charts, graphs and percentages, hold no interest for this hoary professional as he charms spectators to pose at Chatsworth Horse Trials. There is merit in keeping photography simple – 'you need the imagination to free yourself from the gear' advised Terence Donovan. 1971

The Greatest

Yes, there's no doubt in my mind, the title must go to Mrs. Haydon, for I never saw her beaten. In the world of hackney horses she stands supreme. 'Inimitable', 'Outstanding', 'The greatest lady whip of the century' are the opinions advanced when Cynthia Haydon's driving is under discussion.

Even the names of the champions she drove were winners ... how could you better Holywell Florette, Hurstwood Superlative or Highstone Nicholas? With her husband, Frank, an impressive figure – tall, like a guardsman – in close attendance, she was first ... every time.

'There's no People like Show People, They smile when they are low'

The writer and doyen of management consultants, Peter F. Drucker, said something about decisions 'degenerating into work'. Showing horses, producing them to perfection, means careful routine and long hours – and the ability to smile when the judge puts you down the line.

The complete picture – Justine Preston on Royal Tribute. 1994.

Aidan O'Connell

To see Aidan O'Connell showing a horse at Dublin is a treat for those who enjoy the niceties of riding dress. Here he is. Note the double-breasted cut away swallowtail coat, with lining of gold stars, the high collar and matching waistcoat with deep points, the top boots and silver handled whip. Was it true that Beau Brummell had his top boots polished with champagne and peach marmalade? 1997.

Robert Oliver

Another showman who has been at the top of his profession for 25 years, Robert Oliver has successfully combined the summer and winter seasons of showing and foxhunting. At the Royal International Horse Show 1999.

31

Red Coat – Blue Ribband

Allister Hood from Norfolk produces show horses and has headed the line on many occasions. In a profile in Horse and Hound *he said that the balance of feeding, grooming and exercise was the key to success. 'Too many people try to take a short cut. They get two of the basics right, but skimp on the third, usually the exercise. You have to work the horses to build up the muscle.' At the Royal International Horse Show, Allister rides the lightweight hunter Regal Max to win the Winston Churchill Cup. 1996.*

Puttin' on the Ritz

'Come let's mix where Rockefellers walk with sticks
Or umbrellas in their mitts –
Puttin' on the Ritz'

Irving Berlin's greatest rhythmic song seemed just right for Mike
Houghton who, answering a family photocall, looked as though
he was heading for stardom. He holds Mystic Minstrel, his Aunt
Carol Cooper's champion Hack.

Mystic Minstrel

Backgrounds are always difficult for photography at shows, but at the
Horse of the Year Show a spotlight gives me pure black as Carol Cooper's
famous grey Mystic Minstrel, Champion Hack of the Year, leaves the
arena. 1993.

Side-Saddle

I have a book, Modern Side-Saddle Riding *by Eva Christy – 3rd edition revised 1907. It begins by establishing what the sales trainers call 'the buying need'.*

'It has been remarked that nowhere can finer horses be seen than in Hyde Park during the Season. They are the admiration of our Continental visitors, and the subject of frequent comment; but our critics aver that there are only a few really accomplished riders, especially among the ladies'.

After stating the benefits of proper riding technique, the book encourages – 'there is no finer exercise than riding' and 'a woman is said to look her best on horseback, and certainly, when well dressed and well mounted, her figure and carriage are seen to great advantage'.

Few would disagree and, over 90 years on, the Side-Saddle Association has a growing membership to prove it. Its Annual Show at Malvern delights the eye, as young and old strive to join Eva Christy's select band of 'really accomplished riders'.

Cindy Sims

Even if you played cricket, and the Horse and Hound *was a closed book, boys of my age knew there was a girl called Jennifer Skelton who rode ponies, and that she was blonde, with long hair in a single plait. Cindy Sims is her daughter, and when I first photographed her, her hair was long and blonde, and in a single plait. A well-known judge, much in demand today, here she shows a hunter at Windsor.*

Conversation Piece

The Small Riding Horse Class – Windsor, 1999.

The Pony Club Mounted Games

Richard Campbell-Walter, Director of Simpson Piccadilly, sponsors of the Pony Club Mounted Games Championship at Windsor, presents rosettes to the English team, who clearly relish his sense of humour. This competition was started at Windsor in 1980, but the original idea was His Royal Highness The Duke of Edinburgh's. Prince Philip suggested to Colonel Sir Mike Ansell in 1956 that games based on the competitions run for Cavalry Regiments would help train young riders. The Pony Club agreed and the Prince Philip Cup Competition was born.

Gymnastics on Horseback

An interlude among Goodwood's Dressage ... back pads and a padded girth roller with two handles, reveal that these young riders are to give a display of vaulting, a combination of ballet and gymnastics, popular in Germany. To compete, you need to be fit, slim, agile, and probably young – but for some the temptation of sweets and chocolates may prove too great.

The Artist

A surprise, and a refreshing one, to find an artist sketching at Windsor's ringside. This is true art. I cannot think of photography as other than a mechanical process, made even more so by today's press button computer technology. Drawing is another matter and it is no accident that those pre-eminent artists of the horse, Stubbs and Munnings, studied equestrian anatomy at first hand. In Thoughts and Adventures *(1932) Winston Churchill wrote: 'Happy are the painters for they shall not be lonely. Light and colour, peace and hope, will keep them company to the end, or almost to the end of the day.'*

Modern Pentathlete – Katie Houston

'The sort of girl I like to see
Smiles down from her great height at me'

wrote John Betjeman – and

Katie Houston is probably the sort of girl he had in mind. A statuesque Olympian, she is a champion in the Modern Pentathlon. She shoots, fences, swims, rides, runs – and in that order. She was National Champion in 1992 and holds bronze individual and team World Cup medals, and a European team silver. I photographed her in training for the Olympics. 1999.

'Blue Umbrella Sky'

We don't often get what the lyricist and song writer, Johnny Mercer, called a 'blue umbrella sky'. But here's one and Samantha Truscott's grey, her outfit cool in every sense, was irresistible. Hickstead 1999.

Sisters – the Ashbournes

The Ashbourne sisters riding at Ruckley, Shropshire. Away from the main road, the picture reflects the simple pleasure of a convivial summer ride in the English countryside. 1996.

Sisters – the Hennessys

The Hennessy sisters on show hunters. Although Sally on the left usually takes the side-saddle rides, for the picture Moggy is on Roy Creber's famous grey, College Jester, a winner of many championships. 1993.

The Coaching Club

Lt. Col. Sir John Miller, Past President, drives his guests in the grounds of Hampton Court Palace before the Annual Dinner of the Coaching Club. The Club was founded in 1870 and the Duke of Beaufort was President, hence the Club's livery – dark blue coat and buff waistcoat with gilt buttons engraved CC. 1986.

Carriage Horse at Exercise

A snap, no time to focus, as this carriage horse trots by at Windsor. I was struck by the intense colour of the rider's red jersey against the green, on this dull, misty, May morning by the River Thames.

The artist, Augustus John, advised plain apricot for Lord Howard de Walden's racing colours, because it would look well against the green background of the Turf. It did. From the top of the Hurlingham bus, I saw Steve Cauthen in those colours lead from start to finish on Slip Anchor in the 1985 Derby.

His Royal Highness The Duke of Edinburgh

RIGHT: His Royal Highness Prince Philip driving Her Majesty The Queen's Balmoral Fell Ponies in the Harrods International Driving Grand Prix at Windsor in 1996. Having given up polo, Prince Philip looked for something else. Encouraged by the Crown Equerry, Lt. Col. Sir John Miller, and by Major 'Tommy' Thompson, formerly riding master of the Household Cavalry, His Royal Highness took up driving, and was soon competing at International level. His influence on the sport has been incalculable, and that goes for the horse world as a whole since, during his 22 years as President of the FEI, the number of member countries increased from 24 to 85.

BELOW: Passing the Royal Box at Windsor in 1982, the year in which His Royal Highness won the International Driving Championships there. On the Duke's left is David Saunders, his coachman.

Carriage Driving Master –
George Bowman

*George Bowman driving the
obstacle course at Windsor.
His many victories are too
numerous to mention. He is
the most consistent world
class competitor. In cricket,
Jack Hobbs was known as
'The Master'; in the theatre,
it was Noel Coward. In the
world of carriage driving,
there is no doubt the title
belongs to George Bowman.*

First Lady of the Marathon – Karen Bassett

Karen Bassett has crowd appeal. In the marathon, there's anticipation and excitement as she approaches a hazard, then shouts of encouragement as she twists and turns, the sheer physical energy of her horses seems out of proportion to the size of the carriage and the girl in the baseball cap urging them on. Suddenly, she's through and to clapping and cheers she's on to the next. Whip crack away! Windsor 1996.

The Yard Broom

When I looked at this photograph, I could not think what the gentleman with the menacing look was going to do with that yard broom. I'm still far from sure, but the competition at Tatton Park was of the 'fun' variety, to entertain the crowd, and the driver looks as though she's enjoying herself.

Lady Hugh Russell

Crippled as a result of a riding accident, former eventer, Lady Hugh Russell, took up driving. I never cease to admire the way the disabled overcome adversity and achieve an active life in many fields. Rosemary Russell's courage is a perfect example. She straps herself in and drives with dash, skill and enthusiasm.

With Lord Hugh, she made their home Bathampton House, Wylye, Wiltshire, a mecca for eventers, not only for the Horse Trials they pioneered there, but for the training of young riders. She is seen here with her pair of Connemara ponies competing at Tatton Park.

50

Driving Dress

It was the Earl of Chesterfield, founder of the Richmond Driving Club, who insisted that his members 'looked like gentlemen, but drove like coachmen'. In this century, the acknowledged expert on riding dress was Sir Walter Gilbey, who campaigned to raise standards of dress in Rotten Row in the 1930s. At a coaching club meet it was, and still is, correct for gentlemen to wear top hats (either black or grey), and morning coats.

Immaculate turnout is a tradition of carriage driving, which holds good for lady and gentleman drivers today. Sir Walter Gilbey would have approved, but not of the professional on the Guildford coach, referring to one of his subscribers who liked to take the reins – 'I never have a shave on the mornings Mr. _____ is driving, as I always know that I shall get one on the coach.'

51

President of the Coaching Club – John Richards

'A few brave gentlemen, putting back the clock,
A few gallant gentlemen bent on making mock
Of the grim old tyrant, time'

Will H. Ogilvie – White Hats

A leading figure amongst those brave and gallant gentlemen is John Richards, International driver and President of the Coaching Club. Mr. Richards is seen, *with Mrs. Richards beside him, driving his winning team of black Gelderlanders in the Coaching Marathon at Windsor. He wears the cornflower, the emblem of the Coaching Club, and his gleaming coach is a wonderful sight on the eve of the Millennium. I can only raise my glass to him with the traditional driving toast 'The Road'. 1999.*

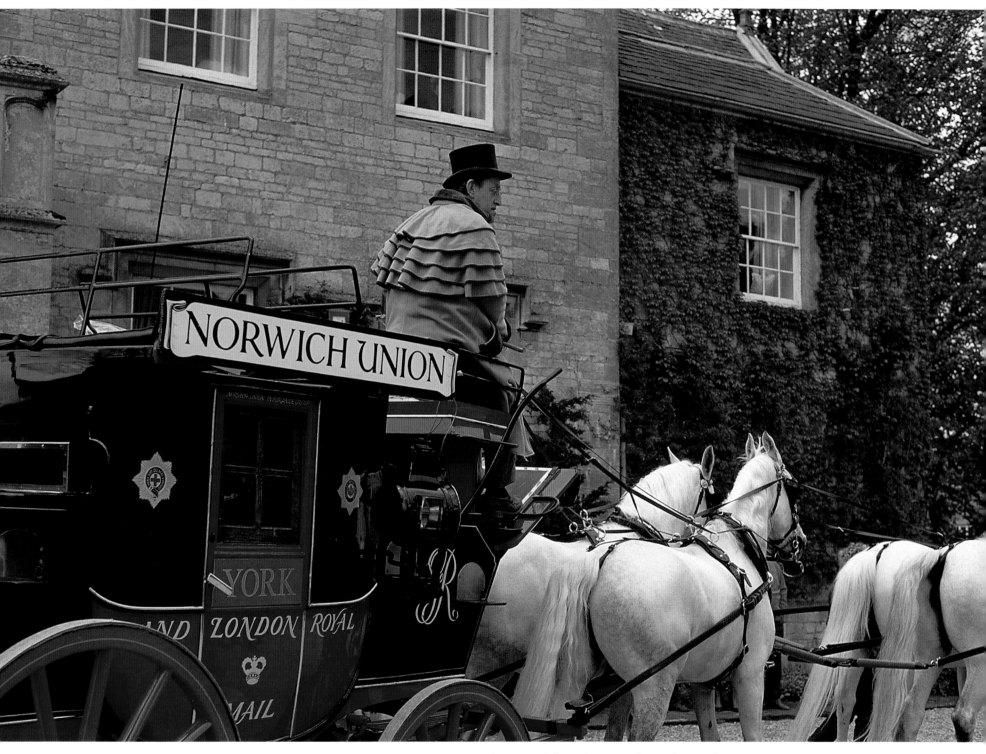

The Norwich Union Coach – John Parker

If you were looking for someone to play the role of professional coachman, there would be no contest, you would merely cast John Parker. With his Dickensian profile, this is one of coaching's characters who looks the part in every way – and plays it, too, for he holds the world record for the 'Quick Change' of a Four-in-Hand team. Here he is at Boothby Hall, Lincolnshire, the home of Lady Netherthorpe.

53

Coaching Hornblower

George Abbott, coaching Hornblower and Ring Guard at Windsor discussing 'The Road' with a fellow coaching hornblower from the United States. George's blowing, a signal to riders to change pace in the show classes at Windsor, lent an old world charm to the occasion. Note he wears a beaver hat of around 1800, a style which was soon to make way for the shining silk toppers of today.

The Mounted Police

Patient and courteous, the mounted branch of the Police always impresses. Their specialised training in this age of mass demonstration is often put to the test. They and their horses are beautifully turned out, and here we have a perfect example, and an Irish horse if I'm not mistaken, on escort duty, on the occasion of the Queen's 60th birthday, Windsor 1986.

55

The Royal Horse Artillery

One Sunday newspaper colour magazine carried a feature suggesting 'the best' designed products in terms of form and function. The ceremonial dress of the King's Troop, Royal Horse Artillery was held to be the best designed uniform in the British Army. And this is it, with a keen-eyed bombardier checking this young gunner's turnout.

The Musical Drive – the King's Troop Royal Horse Artillery

Seventy-six officers, NCOs and Gunners of the King's Troop RHA take part in the musical drive at Royal Windsor Horse Show. The six gun teams (each 20 yards long, with gun and limber weighing 1½ tons) cross the centre of the ring on the diagonal and at full gallop, barely missing each other in the daring 'scissor movement', a breathtaking display of precision riding and pace. The 13-pounder guns are then fired – guns which during World War I were capable of 3 rounds per minute.

The Firing

I was close to this gun – my camera on a sturdy tripod with a standard lens fitted, roughly equivalent to the human eye. The gun went off like thunder. Deafening. The ground shook, camera and tripod leapt in the air, and I did, too, taking the picture in my fright. And this was one gun ...

I thought of the barrage at El Alamein when over 800 guns opened at 9.40 p.m. Could it be true that the Army Commander, as was his habit, had actually gone to bed at 9.00 p.m. and was asleep?

Carriage Horses at Windsor

Coachmen and carriage horses at the Royal Mews, Windsor. Note the intricate and beautiful design of the harness. This is April and the coachmen's dress indicates that showers are expected. Although there are those who wish to sweep away tradition, I marvel that the old skills of coachman and harness maker survive in the century when the motor car took hold and never lost its grip. 1986.

Long service, two medals – Arthur Showell, RVM and Bar

As a Sergeant Riding Instructor in The King's Troop, Royal Horse Artillery, Arthur Showell was awarded the Royal Victorian Medal for his services in charge of the gun team which bore the coffin of King George VI from King's Cross to Westminster for the Lying-in-State in 1952. Nearly forty years later he received a Bar to the medal on his retirement after 23 years as Head Coachman at the Royal Mews. Here he supervises the preparation of carriages at Windsor on The Queen's 60th Birthday. 1986.

Young Coachman – Lofty Perch

The artist Lionel Edwards, writing about state carriages in the Coronation number of Country Life, observed 'I was struck by the height from the ground of the only step onto the coachman's box. It seemed to me that it would require an acrobatic feat to reach it. In fact, the coachman mounts from a step ladder and stays on his lofty perch until the carriage returns to the stables'. A youthful royal coachman on the box, with its hammer-cloth of red and gold, waits before a parade of Royal carriages at Windsor Horse Show. 1986.

Trooping the Colour — Her Majesty The Queen

Her Majesty The Queen, as Colonel-in-Chief Scots Guards, leaves the quadrangle of Buckingham Palace for Horse Guards Parade. The Queen rides in front, and alone. The Colonels of the Household Division, including her husband and eldest son, follow. The photograph implies the loneliness of kingship. Her Majesty rode the black mare Burmese, the gift of the Royal Canadian Mounted Police, on her Birthday Parade for 18 years and this was the last occasion. 1986.

On her 21st Birthday, in a broadcast from Cape Town, South Africa, Her Majesty The Queen, then Princess Elizabeth, vowed:

'I declare before you that my whole life, whether it be long or short, shall be devoted to your service ... '

More than 50 years on, the Queen's dedication remains total. She is the focus of all eyes ... as she was when, in 1949, she rode in the King's Birthday Parade, an immaculate figure in her dark navy uniform as Colonel of the Grenadier Guards, wearing the insignia of the Most Noble Order of the Garter, and riding a fine chestnut horse. In 1951, when she took the salute in place of her father, she opted for an eighteenth century scarlet tunic, with bearskin tricorne and a white cockade.

To ride well side-saddle requires training and the Queen always prepared thoroughly, starting some weeks beforehand. When a youth fired six blank pistol shots at her in 1981, the equestrian world marvelled at her mastery of the art of side-saddle, and her calm control of a prancing horse.

Ascot Week

Applause from the Royal Enclosure as Her Majesty The Queen's carriage arrives at Ascot. The meeting was founded by Queen Anne in 1711 who attended the opening, when all eyes were turned upon Miss Forester, her beautiful Maid of Honour, who was mounted and 'dressed like a man in a long white riding coat, full-flapped waistcoat, court hat bound with gold (point to the front), and a flowing periwig'. 1986.

The Crown Equerry – Lt. Col. Sir John Miller

The Crown Equerry, Lt. Col. Sir John Miller, GCVO, DSO, MC, a highly decorated Welsh Guards officer, holds a press conference at the Royal Mews in 1986. An all-round horseman, who competed at Badminton, Sir John's enthusiasm for, and knowledge of, carriage driving is probably the chief reason why the Royal Mews is home to horses today, and not cars manufactured by Ford.

The Royal Mews flourished under his responsibility as Crown Equerry, 1961-1987. But, in all these years, I guess the high point for him was to ride with The Prince of Wales and the Master of the Horse, The Duke of Beaufort, behind the Gold State Coach, carrying the Queen and Prince Philip to St. Paul's Cathedral on Silver Jubilee Day, 7 June 1977.

The Gold State Coach

The State Coach, 24 feet long and weighing 4 tons, was delivered to the Royal Mews in 1762. It has been used for every Coronation since George IV. Considered for The Queen's Silver Jubilee procession, it was thought to be too slow because the horses can only walk. But Sir John Miller had trained most of the 8 grey horses for driving competitions, they knew his voice and how to walk out. In rehearsal, and with only 'occasional vocal encouragement', the procession reached St. Paul's in record time. So, to everyone's delight, including television world-wide, the Coach was used on the day.

64

Edinburgh

Morning exercise for the Windsor Greys in the park of the Palace of Holyrood House, Edinburgh, in July. They are bound for the wider open spaces of Arthur's Seat, an enjoyable diversion from their Scottish ceremonial duties, where the strict routine and the high standards of the Royal Mews are fully preserved. 1986.

The State Opening of Parliament

The Irish State Coach, followed by the Sovereign's Standard of the Life Guards, catches the November sunlight as it conveys Her Majesty The Queen to the State Opening of Parliament. On the box, is the long-serving *Head Coachman at the Royal Mews, Arthur Showell. This is the height of London pageantry. 1986.*

The Household Cavalry

The Blues and Royals rehearse in Rotten Row before a State visit. The regiment was awarded the status of Household Cavalry for its achievements fighting alongside the Life Guards at Waterloo. The Household Cavalry's special relationship with the Sovereign began in 1678 when King Charles II decreed that, for his personal safety and protection, a Captain commanding the Life Guards should wait upon him, before all others, and should carry an ebony staff with gold head engraved with the Royal Cipher and Crown.

67

The Sovereign's Escort

The Sovereign's Escort 'sit at ease' outside the Palace of Westminster during the State Opening of Parliament. The single helmet with the black plume denotes a Farrier Corporal of Horse in the Life Guards. As we see them, in what used to be called 'Glorious Technicolor', we should remember that these are fighting soldiers. Their Colonel, Field Marshal Lord Allenby, referring to their service in the First World War, said 'they rose to the highest plane of merit, confidently upborne in the knowledge that from those who are greatly trusted great things are due'.

68

The Royal Stables, Oman – His Majesty Sultan Qaboos bin Said

His Majesty Sultan Qaboos bin Said of Oman visits his Royal Stables at Seeb. The prize winners in the Royal Races are paraded before him with the promise of those special sugar lumps received from the Royal Hand. His Majesty The Sultan's Royal Stables embrace many aspects of horsemanship – ceremonial, racing, dressage, showjumping, carriage driving, circus, as well as traditional Arab riding, a heritage which Sultan Qaboos is keen to preserve. His Majesty is a breeder of horses at the Royal Stables, Salalah – and of racing camels at the Royal Camel Stud. 1986.

69

Skill at Arms – Oman

His Majesty Sultan Qaboos bin Said of Oman is a lover of horses and under his guidance horsemanship flourishes at the Royal Stables at Seeb and at Salalah. His Majesty, trained at Sandhurst, makes sure that his Household Mounted Troops, and the Royal Oman Police, are accomplished in traditional Cavalry Skill at Arms. Here, a Royal Stables rider shows his prowess at flag picking. The horse is at full gallop, and has been placed with great accuracy within arm's length of the flag. 1988.

Polo at Smith's Lawn

The British gave the world games – football, certainly. In 1871, when a knock-out competition for the FA Cup was first played, the Morning Post reported on another game:

'Nearly all fashionable London journeyed from Town to Hounslow on Tuesday to witness a new game called "Hockey on Horseback" between the officers of the 9th Lancers and 10th Hussars. Eight players a side, using ash hockey sticks and riding 12.2hh ponies, attempted to hit a white ivory billiard ball.' The report continued 'it was admitted by all who were looking on that it was more remarkable for the strength of the language used by the players, than for anything else'.

Master and Huntsman – Major Bob Field Marsham

Major Bob Field Marsham belonged to that band of dedicated soldier foxhunters who kept hunting going in the difficult days during and after the Second World War. Tall and angular, he was an inspiring figure, as well as a much respected breeder and judge of hounds. He was Master of the Bicester, but my photograph shows him with the Eridge in 1960.

'A Good Game for Conversation'

The incomparable Henry Longhurst, in a tribute to Winston Churchill, wrote that the great man once declared that golf was 'a good game for conversation'. Masters may discourage it at covert side, but hunting is another 'good game for conversation', especially as here, at a meet of the Quorn 1998.

The Quorn – Patrick Gee

My father-in-law, Patrick Gee, (in top hat) with the Quorn. He had been driven 100 miles to the meet by his daughter, and is enjoying agreeable conversation. Note the hairy obstacle, which could prove to be the first fence. Scholar, soldier, farmer, solicitor and magistrate, he came to Leicestershire late and was near three score years and ten in this photograph. Although he described himself as a 'carpetbagger', he swapped Essex plough for the grass of the Shires and never looked back. 1970.

Leicestershire – the Rolls-Royce

The racing driver, Tony Brooks, after testing the Rolls-Royce Silver Cloud, summed up: 'As a big, luxurious car that can nevertheless be driven in a highly sporting manner, there is nothing quite like it.' This gentleman took his Cloud to Leicestershire – and what could be more highly sporting than that?

The Quorn – Michael Farrin

BELOW: Michael Farrin proved an inspired choice when he was put on as huntsman to the Quorn at the early age of 24. Thirty years later, and in his last season, he moves off from a Friday Meet. Note the gentle, undulating country. No wonder Beatrice Holden would write 'those happy hunting grounds, my friend, the SHIRES'. 1998.

ABOVE LEFT: Drawing crowds and cameras at his retirement presentation meet – 1998 and (ABOVE RIGHT) as a young huntsman at the start of his career.

Quenby Hall

'The Stately Homes of England, how beautiful they stand ... ' Soft winter sunlight plays on Quenby, one of the finest houses in the Quorn country, and the home of many famous foxhunters, including Sir Harold Nutting, Bart., Master of the Quorn throughout the 1930s. The present owner is Squire de Lisle, Chairman of the Hunt. 1998.

Second Horses – The Quorn

There is a sense of urgency as two gentlemen in scarlet change horses, keen not to miss a moment of a Quorn Friday in 1998.

F.E. Smith, the first Earl of Birkenhead, said that one of his ambitions was to be a really good man to hounds ... 'a man like Arthur Thatcher, never faltering, never hesitating, never flustered'. Thatcher, Huntsman to the Fernie and the Cottesmore, was a legendary figure, but the definition applies equally to the horse sports of today, and to great games players, too.

The Fernie

I always wanted to capture something of a Lionel Edwards painting on film. Not easy, and I tried many times, but this is my best attempt. The huntsman is Bruce Durno. Alas, there is no 'Lionel Edwards Sky', for mine is as flat as studio seamless. Still, I like to think that 'L.E.', master artist of the hunting field, would have given me credit for trying.

The Map

A map comes in useful during a morning's cub-hunting with the Beaufort from Easton Grey. Folding pocket hunt maps were once easily obtainable. Mine was waterproofed, I remember. 1986.

The Beaufort at Worcester Lodge

Captain Ian Farquhar, Master and Huntsman, leads his field from Worcester Lodge, the splendid building at the north end of Badminton park, designed by William Kent for the 3rd Duke of Beaufort in the eighteenth century. It is the Opening Meet and poppies denote Remembrance Sunday is near. Event riders should drink a toast to the memory of the 10th Duke of Beaufort, known as Master from the day he was given his own pack of harriers by his father at the age of 11. His love of horses and hunting persuaded him to run the first Three Day Event at Badminton in 1949.

The Blue and Buff

The fashionable and the famous, including the Duke of Windsor as Prince of Wales, Prince Charles and Princess Anne have worn the Blue and Buff, the personal livery of the Dukes of Beaufort which goes back generations at Badminton. A foggy Saturday at Easton Grey, and a delayed start, gave me the chance to photograph this immaculate wearer, a model of correct hunting dress.

Hunting Man

It's late in the day, but Captain Farquhar of the Beaufort will draw again to be sure his big Saturday field gets fair value. Certain to be with them is a fine figure in a swallowtail coat, with rather special experience of the country around Badminton – Olympic Gold Medallist Richard Meade.

The End of the Day – the Beaufort

*The end of the day and, from the steaming horses, a good run, too. This is
the Beaufort field on a Saturday near Didmarton. 1991.*

84

The Great Meet

The combined Leicestershire packs meet on Melton Airfield to protest against anti-hunting legislation. Lord Kimball alerts the organisers to a cheque, a donation to a well-known charity. The argument rages about hunting. Captain Burns Hartopp, appointed Master of the Quorn in 1898, said at his first General Meeting, he presumed hunting was for fun, and he should do his best to show them some. Sad that fun should be denied, but fun it is, and always was. Perhaps that's the problem.

Yet hunting has deep roots in the country. In February 1852 at Strathfieldsaye, and a few months before his death at 83, the Duke of Wellington wrote to a friend:

'I understand we are to have the Hounds here, which may detain me for some hours, as I conclude the people will not be satisfied if I should not take a gallop with them'.

Going out at Cheltenham – Tony McCoy

Tony McCoy, the champion jockey, going out at Cheltenham. With 134 winners for the season already, he is at the top of his profession, the toughest in sport. But he knows that another champion, the trainer Martin Pipe, has prepared his horse for this race and that he was the son of a bookmaker, who 'liked to get the odds in his favour'. 1999.

The Champion Hurdle – jubilant winner, gallant loser

'It has to be Istabraq' ran the headline – and it was. Shouts of 'Charlie, Charlie!' greet Charlie Swan and Istabraq after retaining the Champion Hurdle title in 1999. But the picture is poignant, for there are no cheers for Istabraq's stablemate Theatreworld, who steals away, runner up for the third successive year, as jockey Tommy Treacy reflects on what might have been. These great rivals, thrilling the Festival crowds, are bred to the highest class. Both horses are by Sadler's Wells, a son of the world famous sire Northern Dancer.

'Talent is beautiful' – the Bullen family

Top Right: The Bullen family has talent and, as Irving Berlin said 'talent is beautiful'. Michael and his sisters, Jennie and Jane, have a remarkable record. Michael rode in the Three Day Event at the Rome Olympics in 1960. My picture shows him on Colonel V.D.S. Williams' Cottage Romance, his Olympic ride, at Badminton in 1961.

Jane repeated the feat in Mexico in 1968 winning a team gold medal, having won Badminton on Our Nobby in April, when the press hailed her as 'the Galloping Nurse'. On Warrior, she was to win Burghley in 1976 and Badminton in 1978, a rare double.

Below Left: Jennie won a bronze medal in the World Dressage Championships at Goodwood in 1978 on her famous stallion Dutch Courage, the highest placed British competitor ever.

Below Right: Jane Bullen, before the cross-country start at Chatsworth, with her sisters Jennie and Sarah. She is on Blue Danube, with owner Miss Profumo at right. Sarah was another fine rider who became an actress. She was in her element when she played the part of an eventer in the film International Velvet.

Going fast for Olympic Gold
– Laurie Morgan

The Australian Olympic Gold Medallist, Laurie Morgan, after winning Badminton on Salad Days, his Olympic champion, in 1961. This was his lap of honour, taken at a steady walk. Today's orgy of self-congratulation, the fist punching the air, the hysterical gallop, followed by hugs and kisses, was not his style. An all-round horseman and twice winner of the Foxhunters' at Aintree over the Grand National fences, he would write of the cross-country phase, 'when you think you are going fast, go faster, and make a certainty of getting the maximum effort from your horse'.

The Gladiator

Susan Fleet, with The Gladiator, had a fine record in one day horse trials, but was unplaced at Badminton. As the country emerged from the snowbound winter of 1962–3 and Badminton was confined to a One Day *Event, she seized her chance and won. The Gladiator lived up to his name and triumphed in fearful conditions as horses struggled in relentless driving rain and Badminton mud. But here it looks easy – Tidworth 1961.*

The Gunner who won Gold – Staff Sergeant Ben Jones, RHA

Long ago, at Badminton and Tidworth, a wiry horse gunner with a lean drawn face caught my eye. Staff Sergeant Ben Jones of The King's Troop Royal Horse Artillery was taking on the officers and beating them, rare for an NCO in the 1960s when the Colonels were in charge. But his talent took him to two Olympic Games and a Team Gold Medal in Mexico. He taught Mary Gordon-Watson and inspired her success with Cornishman. And all this, while a serving soldier. We should remember him. Here he is on Sherpa at Badminton. 1961.

Anneli Drummond-Hay

ABOVE: A soaring leap by Merely-a-Monarch, the mount of Anneli Drummond-Hay at Badminton in 1962. The horse trounced its rivals in an awesome display of all-round athleticism and power. It is doubtful that a horse could so dominate Badminton again, but you can only beat the best in the world in your day, and the tall girl on the matchless 'Monarch' showed how it's done. They won Burghley in the same year and, having beaten everyone, retired to the showjumping arena at international level, and further success.

RIGHT: At Hickstead, 35 years later, on a visit from South Africa – and still looking the part.

Gurgle the Greek

Rachel Bayliss gallops to the finishing post on her famous eventer, Gurgle the Greek, an outstanding combination 25 years ago. Almost unbeatable in One Day Events, they made the record books at Badminton in 1973 when 'Gurgle', without penalty, went under, rather than over, the Stockholm fence, forcing a change in the rules.

A Fall

A horse weighs half a ton and, looking at this photograph, it's a terrifying thought ... but the rider was thrown clear and, much to my relief, was up and on her way again in a matter of seconds.

National Hero, genial host – The Marquess of Exeter

At the 440 yards, over 3-feet hurdles, the then Lord Burghley was unsurpassed in his generation ... and a national hero when he won the gold medal in the 1928 Olympics in Amsterdam. He set many records and won more than 100 races.

But horsemen knew him as a smiling, genial host at Burghley. Crippled with arthritis, I can see him rising to his feet, no doubt painfully, to return

the salute of every competitor who rode past him in the parade before the showjumping. After his first of two hip replacement operations, Lady Exeter had the hip-joint silver plated by Garrards and mounted on his Rolls-Royce (number plate AAA1). He is shown with competitors on dressage day, before the era of top hat and tails, on the occasion of the first running of Burghley Horse Trials in 1961. The riders are Jean Sansome on Nutmeg, Lt. Peter Hervey 15th/19th The King's Royal Hussars on High Jinks and Gay Tilney on Leander.

First Champion of Europe – Sheila Willcox

Although she would later opt for this chequered crash hat, Sheila Willcox wore a plain black velvet hunting cap for dressage, for cross-country, and for showjumping when she won Badminton in 1957 on High and Mighty at the age of 21. In the same year, she made history by being the first woman to become European Champion. She won Badminton again on High and Mighty in 1958 and, to underline her riding talent, scored a third victory on Airs and Graces in 1959.

THE
FIELD
THE BEST
FOR
COUNTRY
SPORT
EVERY
THURSDAY 3°

Reflections before the Start

What thoughts cram the mind before the cross-country start? The course is walked, so you know every ditch and drop, twist and turn. At Chatsworth, Sally Strachan chose to have a few moments alone before her number was called.

Individual Olympic Gold Medallist – Richard Meade

It comes as a surprise that, with so much post war British interest in the Three Day Event, we can claim only one individual Olympic gold Medallist. He is Richard Meade OBE. He rode in four Olympic Games and had the honour of carrying the Union Jack and leading the British contingent into the arena. A perfect stylist who went foxhunting to prepare horses for the cross-country, he rode a succession of 'greats' – Barberry, Cornishman, The Poacher and Laurieston, his Olympic Gold Medal winner. Here he rides Flamingo for Lady Hugh Russell at Badminton. 1971.

Her Royal Highness Princess Anne

The horse world was thrilled when HRH Princess Anne, riding Doublet, won the European Three Day Event Championship at Burghley in 1971. On Goodwill, she would compete in the Montreal Olympics in 1976. She has been a tireless ambassador for equestrian causes and followed her father as President of the FEI.

Her prowess and regular appearance as a rider in Horse Trials widened public interest in the sport in the early 1970s.

Eventing Master – Mark Phillips

Her Royal Highness Princess Anne, who was fifth on Doublet, looks on as Lt. Mark Phillips steps forward to receive his first Whitbread Trophy at Badminton in 1971. A high ranking member of Badminton's army of officials and helpers holds Great Ovation, a former show horse, who won again the following year, adding an Olympic Team Gold Medal to his tally.

As writer, teacher and course builder, multiple Badminton winner Mark Phillips is an eventing 'Master'. Were he a golfer, he would certainly wear the green jacket of Augusta National. What more prestigious job in eventing could there be than trainer to the United States Three Day Event Team?

Caroline Bradley

Caroline Bradley rode in One Day Events before coming to fame as a showjumper. Here she approaches the first fence on the cross-country with an eye for a proper take-off, which would later serve her so well. Her early death, at the age of 37, was mourned throughout the horse world.

Girl of Steel – Mary Gordon-Watson

I can see the Sunday paper headline now 'Gallant horse – Girl of Steel' ... the horse was Cornishman V, and the girl was Mary Gordon-Watson. The story was that they won the World Three-Day Event Championship in 1970. Mary, already European Champion, was what used to be called 'a slip of a gel' – but steel, yes. Cornishman was a mighty 17hh, some horse. Together they won Team Gold Medals at European and Olympic level. Here she weighs in at Badminton 1971. The following year, she won a team Gold Medal in the Olympics at Munich, placed fourth overall.

'Energy is eternal delight' – Bruce Davidson

Bruce Davidson, athletic, golden-haired, American, was in his country's Three-Day Event Team at the age of 22. At 24, he was World Champion. Twenty-five years later he's still posting his entry for Badminton. Year after year he has come to England to compete and we are lucky to have him. His love of horses – breeding, training and riding them over three decades at the highest level is unmatched. 'Energy is eternal delight ...' wrote Blake – and to horsemen everywhere Bruce Davidson is America's living proof. Burghley 1984.

The Olympian –
Portrait of Mark Todd

The New Zealand Three - Day Event rider, Mark Todd, belongs to a very exclusive club – those who have won Individual Olympic Gold Medals in successive Games. He is a wizard on a horse. He has proved this many times, not least when he jumped on Horton Point, a chance ride, the day before Badminton 1994 and won. This photograph was taken at Burghley in 1984.

Perfect Production – Ginny Elliot

Ginny Elliot's event horses were beautifully produced. No detail was overlooked by a production crew worthy of the Great British Director himself, David Lean. And Ginny's mother, Heather Holgate, and trainer Dot Willis, produced Oscar-winning performances from their star rider.

On a succession of meticulously prepared horses, her three wins at Badminton, five at Burghley, and her team Silver and individual Bronze medals at the 1984 and 1988 Olympics proved the value of teamwork, and looks a record hard to beat. She is seen leaving the arena on Nightcap, her 1984 Burghley winner, and about to trot up Murphy Himself before their 1986 triumph.

Teenage idol, eventing Superstar – Lucinda Prior-Palmer

Horse-mad teenagers flocked to Badminton in the 1970s to catch a glimpse of the sport's undoubted superstar, Lucinda Prior-Palmer. They were well rewarded. She had that magic something which made her more exciting to watch. She rode with smiling dash, she adored her horses and it showed. The crowds loved her, cheering her to a record victory on six different horses at Badminton, as well as European and World titles. She called her autobiography Up, Up and Away, *which defined her cross-country style.*

The Trout Hatchery

The water draws the biggest crowd on the cross-country course – the spectacle of a rider taking a ducking is too good to miss. But I never cease to admire the unfailing good humour of competitors when disaster strikes. This is Clarissa Strachan at the Burghley Trout Hatchery. Her charming smile conceals her inner feelings as she faces 60 penalties with Delphy Kingfisher, and a sodden, saddle-slithery, ride ahead. 1979.

The thrill of winning – Mary Thomson

Mary Thomson (now Mrs. King) looked the part in every way. Tall, slim, she wore her clothes beautifully and rode gorgeous horses. Among eventers, she acquired supermodel status in the early 90s. She had an easy, smiling way with her. You wanted to look at her. You felt she would have succeeded in any field, but she chose horses and went to the top. Above all, she enjoyed it as I think my picture, taken at Badminton, shows.

She is on King Boris, her British Open Champion 'with the tail like a propeller'. 1988.

She won Badminton – 'the cream of the cream of our sport' in 1992 on King William. After a second and a third in the great event, to win was magic – 'nothing like coming second' said Mary, and everyone in competitive sport will know what she means.

Badminton in the Spring

LEFT: Alas, so often rain intervenes to ruin one of the biggest sporting spectacles in the country. A year to remember was 1961, but these young admirers asked, and Michael Bullen obliged.

ABOVE: The park at Badminton as we would wish to see it during the Championship in early May.

Madeleine Gurdon

Madeleine Gurdon (now Lady Lloyd-Webber) was a top eventer in the 1980s. She has since become well-known as an owner and breeder of race horses. Horses are in her blood, and that is as it should be for one who has the distinction of wearing the Union Jack pocket badge on her swallowtail coat. Here she is competing at Burghley on Midnight Monarch II. 1986.

Generous

Generous won the Derby and this is a good name for a horse. As a mere bystander, I have been struck by the generous way event horses jump. They try valiantly as they are, in the jargon, 'asked questions'. They leap with an accuracy and balance which, in human terms, is reserved only for the gymnasium or the ballet. Here's a generous horse trying for all he's worth at Chatsworth.

The Veterinary Inspection

What used to be a rather informal affair has now become something of a show, even a fashion show. At Burghley, Michael Tucker is seen with officials (including the 1970 Burghley winner Judy Bradwell), as he prepares to trot up General Bugle. A lifelong eventing enthusiast, and now a broadcaster on the sport, Michael Tucker and his wife Angela have seen the tremendous growth in Horse Trials over the past thirty years at first hand, and from the saddle. 1986.

Collecting Ring View

Competitors watch final day showjumping at Burghley. Eventing is like championship golf, in that you don't know if you have won until the final round is over. Misfortune strikes and in an instant you can drop down the order, losing a prize, or even the Gold Medal. 1984.

113

'Hunting Mothers and Daughters'

ABOVE: For a magazine article on 'Hunting Mothers and Daughters', Polly joins her sister Tessa and mother, Lady Clark, after a day's hunting with Sir Watkin Williams Wynn's. Polly admits her eventing success, on many different horses, owes much to lessons learned in the hunting field.

Success with a silver lining – Polly Clark

BELOW: Polly Clark's eventing year 1998 had a touch of Grand Slam about it. Champion at Windsor, Bramham and Blenheim, on three different horses, the silver haul was impressive. The sumptuous Windsor trophy in the centre seems to belong to another era and one wonders what the value 'for insurance' would be if it featured on the Antiques Road Show. *1999.*

The Nations' Cup – The Aga Khan Trophy

Twenty-six years separate these Dublin photographs, but some showjumping legends are here. In 1970, the British team comprised David Broome on Sportsman, Ann Moore on Psalm, Stephen Hadley on No Reply and Graham Fletcher on Buttevant Boy, who lost the Cup to Germany by a quarter of a fault.

In 1996, the team of Di Lampard, Nick Skelton, Robert Smith and John Whitaker won. For me, it was a bright gleam on a sombre afternoon for photography, even if the face of John Whitaker, holding the Cup, gives no hint of his team's triumph.

115

Flying the Flag – Nona Garson

Nona Garson, from Lebanon, New Jersey, began riding at the age of five, rising steadily through the ranks of pony and junior jumper classes to Grand Prix level and the US Equestrian Team on horses she trained herself.

Here she greets cheering fans during the Nations' Cup Parade of Teams, her flashing smile and all-embracing wave contrasts with the steadfast regimental gaze of the soldier who has the honour to bear Old Glory, the United States flag. Dublin 1997.

Show Jumping – Ireland wins

Captain John Ledingham holds the gold Aga Khan Trophy aloft after Ireland's victory in the Nation's Cup. His team members are from left to right, Eddie Macken, Trevor Coyle and Paul Darragh. And, with 1500 horses passing through the gates of the RDS Ballsbridge, it seems right that Ireland should win on the big day, when the ring stewards wear top hats and tails, and the President attends. Dublin 1997.

'You only have one chance' – Di Lampard

Britain's leading lady showjumper, Di Lampard, trained with Caroline Bradley. A veteran of 25 years on the circuit, her career highlights include winning the first of two Queen Elizabeth II Cups on Abbervail Dream, when the horse was only seven, and her Bronze medal at the World Equestrian Games in Rome in 1998. In 1999, she became the first lady to win the Cock o'the North trophy at Harrogate, beating the Yorkshiremen on their home ground. A formidable competitor, she stresses concentration – 'you only have one chance – there's no re-run'. At Hickstead 1999.

Aachen – a class act

LEFT: Aachen is a class act in dressage and show-jumping. For the people of Aachen, like the people of Augusta during Masters week, it is their show, and 1998 was the Centenary year. My picture shows Mark Armstrong on Primma jumping a fence advertising Mercedes Benz, sponsors since 1954. Note TV screen at right recording the action.

BELOW: Dressage riders in the Aachen arena. 1998.

Her Royal Highness Princess Haya

Her Royal Highness Princess Haya of Jordan is an international showjumper who competes at top shows. Based in Germany, she is seen here at Dublin in 1996.

Rotten Row

'Nothing could ever break or harm
The charm of London Town'

wrote Noël Coward, and one of its charms is surely Rotten Row.

A shaft of early morning sun rimlights the figure of a lone rider with only joggers for company. The 'Route du Roi' was a carriage road planned by William III to Kensington Palace, but it was not until the Regency that riding in the park became fashionable. 1998.

The Man in a Hurry

Most riders in the Row settle for a leisurely pace, but nothing short of a full blown gallop will do for this intrepid young man. I wondered what was going through his mind as he sped past me. Was he a City banker, frustrated in the middle of a big deal? Or did he imagine he was in the final furlong at Epsom? No, I guess he was just having fun, which is what Rotten Row is for. 1998.

'A Leisurely Pace ...'

Household Cavalry Drum horses at exercise in Hyde Park 1998.

122

A ride in Windsor Great Park

A cool blonde, with free-flowing hair – I feel Alfred Hitchcock would have cast Lally Waddington – here enjoying a summer evening ride in Windsor Great Park. 1996.

On Dartmoor

July, and a brooding Dartmoor sky, but what a view. A wonderful place, away from 'the roaring traffic's boom', and even if you have to pick your way on those rocky hills, you come close to nature with only a horse for company. 1996.

Mountain Greenery

'On the first of May
It is moving day;
Spring is here, so blow your job –
Throw your job away ...'

Throwing his job away, is dressage horse Jack. Hours of winter pounding –
extensions, half halts and half passes, even piaffe – lie behind him, for this
is his first day at grass.

'Eat and you'll grow fatter, boy
S'matter, boy?
Atta boy!'

Yes, the lyrics of Lorenz Hart come to mind as Jack blesses his mountain
greenery home. 1999.

Mare and Foal – a good place to be born

The foal shows the inquisitive characteristics of youth, while his mother (who has seen it all before) pays no attention. 'What is this strange fellow doing?' thinks the youngster. I wonder about him, and what will become of him. But I know he's in good hands for this is Beaufort country, just across the park from Badminton ... and if you're a horse, that's a very good place to be born.

The Show Horse – a day off

Turned out for the afternoon, a well-bred show horse canters delightedly around his field. Horses stand in stables for so long that their pleasure in finding sudden freedom is a joy to watch. 1992.

'Don't forget to use the fog!'

My American mentor, the New York photographer Lucille Khornak, signing her book 'Fashion Photography' for me, wrote 'Don't forget to use the fog!' This attempt shows Alison Murray Wells exercising on a misty morning at Shipton Moyne, Gloucestershire, and I hope Lucille would approve. 1986.

Timeless side-saddle

Claire Proctor was modelling for me and I asked her to pause at the front door. The portrait has a timeless quality about it. It was taken in Yorkshire and reminded me of a favourite Lionel Edwards, a meet of the Bramham Moor at Bickerton Bar, painted in 1927 for the book More Shires and Provinces. *There are elegant ladies riding side-saddle and on foot – and I felt Claire might be just off to join them. 1992.*

Two Pioneers

Mrs. Lorna Johnstone, a tremendous all-round horsewoman, hunted in Yorkshire as a child and showed a 13.2hh pony at Olympia in 1912, before going to India, where she broke ponies to ride and to stick and ball. Her dressage career began when she attended a course given by Monsieur Cuyer in 1935. 25 years later, when her contemporaries had long settled for the rocking chair, she rode in the Olympic Games.

Mrs. V.D.S. Williams did much to widen interest in dressage after the war. She was a fine all-rounder who played tennis for Shropshire and golf for South Staffordshire, but she won the admiration of all when she represented Great Britain at dressage in two Olympic Games. Here, riding Little Model, she leaves the ring after one of her many demonstrations.

The youthful, talented, ambitious, dressage riders of today, with their eye on the Olympic Games, should spare a thought for these two great ladies who led the way.

130

Watching Dressage – a serious business

It is May, but it seems 'Spring will be a little late this year ...' Nothing daunts the dressage watcher. It is a serious business. Early starts are often called for, and long distances travelled, to catch 7 minutes of a favoured rider in the arena. Windsor 1997.

Dressage – 'high achievement, great pleasure and good exercise'

Anthony Crossley once wrote of dressage: 'Half an acre of land, one horse, no groom and less than an hour a day are the modest essential requirements for high achievement, great pleasure and good exercise. And all those good things can be indulged in five or six days a week all the year round and up to a very ripe old age'. One who would agree is Claire Kok, wearing her Shell Gas Tee Shirt, big sponsors of dressage in the early 1990s, and demonstrating the half pass.

Goodwood – see the coat tails fly

Colonel Alois Podhajsky, of the Spanish Riding School, called his autobiography My Dancing White Horses *and this photograph, the girl on the grey in joyful canter, coat tails flying, reminds me of a Viennese waltz. And it recalls happy days as a casual snapshooter at what came to be known as Goodwood Dressage, thanks to the generous patronage of the Earl and Countess of March, who founded this matchless event in the grounds of their home.*

Goodwood – working in

The outside arenas at Goodwood, where the best in the world 'worked in', were full of interest. 'We only remember the sunny hours' but the sun did shine at Goodwood, although I do remember a fearful midsummer storm, with hailstones nearly the size of the proverbial golf balls.

'Full swing in the half-pass'

LEFT: Anthony Crossley's caption for this photograph on the back cover of his book Advanced Dressage *(Stanley Paul 1982). And full swing it is, for this is the Swiss rider, Christine Stückelberger, and the unique Granat, Olympic and World Champions. Goodwood 1978.*

France triumphant – Margit Otto-Crépin

Riding for France during the Goodwood years was Margit Otto-Crépin. A slight blonde figure, she is seen here on her No. 1 horse, the powerful Corlandus, who is like a coiled spring with his rider just beginning to show some pre-test tension.

Ten minutes later, it's all smiles as Corlandus leaves the ring, having delighted Margit, and shown the big match temperament that a dressage champion needs. Together they were unbeatable at Goodwood 1987 – 1989, and won the Olympic Silver Medal in Seoul 1988.

Anni MacDonald-Hall

Anni MacDonald-Hall came to the fore in the 1980's. She was new to dressage and her progress was rapid to the point where she, too, was signing her name like a film star.

Goodwood's long-serving Steward – David Braham

Visitors to Goodwood Dressage, whether riders or spectators, will remember David Braham, the ever present and watchful steward. Throughout the lifespan of the Championships – the 20 years 1973–1993 – Mr. Braham, dark suited with bowler hat, kept things running with gentlemanly charm.

Here he inspects the bridlework of the Austrian rider Regina Moldan. David Braham is a fine example of those who freely give their time to make horse events possible – and this is a way of saying 'thank you'.

The Indoor School

A skylight turns available darkness into available light. Just enough to take a photograph of this competitor using the mirror to check her position in this indoor school at Waregem, Belgium. On the continent, where dressage is a way of life, the indoor riding school has proved invaluable for year round training.

139

Dressage in a garden – Diane Hogg and Barrollo

ABOVE: At Windsor, the grass dressage arena, set apart from the main showground and against a backcloth of fine Spring foliage, is unique. It gives the effect of dressage in a garden, and a Royal garden at that. On her way to winning the 1999 Grand Prix, and the Kur, is Diane Hogg on Barrollo. Diane has won six international classes with Barrollo, bought as a five-year-old from a local riding school, in response to an advertisement in the Farmers Guardian.

RIGHT: First in line – Hickstead 1998.

Fitness and Competence

'In the interests of the horse, the fitness and competence of the rider shall be regarded as essential' states Clause 7 in the Code of Conduct for Dressage issued by the FEI. This was put to the test when Ferdi Eilberg's Broadstone Warianka, having won first prize, decided a mild celebration in the form of high jinks was called for. Her rider fully proved his 'fitness and competence'. With no stirrups, and with a horse rug over the saddle, he remained unmoved, while Carl Hester, the runner-up, looked on. Stoneleigh 1998.

Evening Light

International Dressage-riders wait before their prize-giving at Waregem,
Belgium in warm evening sunlight.

Black is Chic

The Russian dressage rider Inessa Poturajeva schooling Targim at Aachen. The way the so-called weaker sex ride and train these horses, which are certainly in the officer's charger, if not the heavy-weight hunter category, amazes me. Inessa is wearing what I suppose is the rider's equivalent of 'the little black dress'. She is lightness and chic – the horse, generous and willing. 1998.

Aachen Elegance

The Dutch rider, Coby van Baalen and Olympic Ferro show some of the stylish elegance associated with dressage at Aachen. 1998.

A Special Relationship

To train a dressage horse to international level takes years. How many 'flying hours' in the log book, I wonder? A bond must develop. This photograph shows an intimate moment. Hickstead 1998.

The Dressage trainer – David Hunt

For thirty years, David Hunt has been at the forefront of British Dressage – as international competitor, notably with his Grand Prix winner Maple Zenith, as administrator, and as judge. But it is as a trainer that he is best

known. He is tireless. He will start his first pupil at 7.00 a.m. and finish twelve hours later, with only the shortest break for lunch. Young and old drive miles for 45 minutes with David. Here, he has a final word with Sarah Dwyer, Louise Francis and Ann Marie Hancock before a quadrille at Goodwood.

Equestrian Fashion

My interest in equestrian fashion developed after I attended several photo-workshops in the United States. The story goes that David Bailey and Terence Donovan attempted to list what could go wrong in a fashion shoot, and when they reached four hundred, they stopped counting. So fashion photography is hard enough, but add horses and the problems multiply.

Emma Wilkinson was perfect for this cover shot. Only a horsewoman could tie a stock like that, and she looks as though she was poured into that coat. Immaculate. 1989.

147

The Studio Background – Katie Moore

Katie Moore, a leading producer and rider of show hacks, chose this location near her home and give me a big sky background, as though we were in a huge photographic studio.

The Sombrero

Amanda James looked wonderful and rode beautifully. A threatening Northampton sky was hardly right for a sombrero picture but we snatched this before the rain fell. 1992.

149

Bond Street in the Stable

Amanda James wears the latest. To me, this looks a bit like Bond Street, but why not? 1993.

The Tailor-made Coat

Samantha Roberts poses at Windsor for a photoguide on showing dress. This is a very neat, understated outfit, a model to copy. 1998.

'Buy the Best'

'Correct turnout is part of the whole presentation of the horse to the Judge ... Do buy the best you can afford, both in clothes and riding boots. In the long run, this is a most sound investment. The quality of material, the cut and fit make a tremendous difference to the overall picture' wrote Ruth McMullen in Simpson's booklet on Correct Riding Clothes 1978. This was before Rebecca Miller was born, but she proves the theory in this picture. 1998.

Pretty Ponies and Buttons and Bows

'And I'm all yours in buttons and bows ...' sang Bob Hope in The Paleface *and* Buttons and Bows *won the 1948 Oscar for Best Song. Now Hollywood has come to Hickstead. Yes, buttons and bows abound in the Leading Rein Class. And the colour is chiefly red. Anxious mothers watch from ringside as professional trainers, dressed for a garden party rather than a gallop, lead the way. But, who knows ... we may have a future Olympic Gold Medallist here. 1999.*

The Riding Habit

This riding habit c.1790–1800 was made by Lucy Nickless as part of her BA Honours course in Costume for the Screen and Stage at Bournemouth & Poole College of Art & Design. The model is Jemma Harding, a former member of the Bronze Medal-Winning British Ponies, Dressage Team. 1998.

154

The Three-cornered Hat

One of the most attractive hats is the tricorne. In the eighteenth century, ladies wore men's three-cornered hats for riding, just as in later years they would adopt top hats and bowlers. I wish the tricorne would reappear more often, but I caught these members of the Iberian Horse Quadrille at Windsor. 1996.

Dressage – the swallowtail coat

The black swallowtail coat is a severe garment, but Claire Kok invests it with statuesque beauty, form and figure. Wiltshire 1992.

Tall in the saddle

Equestrian models seem to stand 5' 12" these days. This is dressage rider Emma Wright, and I trust she will forgive me if I call her the perfect clotheshorse.

Finding models isn't easy – they must be the right shape (the camera puts on 7lbs), able to ride well, and wear the clothes with style. 'She's not the girl next door, she's the girl you wished lived next door' said David Bailey.

Blonde Beauty

'CHIO – Sales – the top horses of tomorrow' ran the headline in the Aachen Media Guide. Throughout the show, 24 Rhineland and Westfalia-bred horses, between three and six years were presented in the arena by elegant riders, casual yet stylish. Seeing this blonde beauty, I stole a fashion picture. 1998.

Polly Lyon

A wide brimmed magenta hat added colour when Polly Lyon, a former European Young Rider Three-Day Event Individual Gold Medallist, agreed to model. Polly wears breeches of blue denim. Diana Vreeland, the high priestess of American fashion and editor-in-chief of Vogue, was hesitatingly asked 'What do you think of ... er ... blue jeans?' 'They're the most beautiful things since the gondola' came the swift reply. 1994.

159

'Sticky Bum' breeches

But what would Mrs. Vreeland have said about 'sticky bum' breeches ... do they really help? 1993.

Inborn Elegence – Nickette Finlan

Nickette, half French, has inborn elegance. A high fashion horsewoman, she showed her big, beautiful, Irish hunters with dash and style – she looked divine, and was my first model. 1984.

The brown Top Hat

Catherine Smallbone, the New Zealand dressage rider, tries on a brown top hat, a perfect match with her shirt. She thought better of the purchase, no doubt because the dressage rule book states 'Top hat with black/dark blue coat'. 1998.

The Amazons

Designers are looking at riding wear, reviving old ideas and coming up with new ones. As the historian of costume James Laver wrote: 'Riding is not only a matter of the show ring, it is also a scamper over the Downs, or even along the unfrequented shore. It would be a great pity if the shibboleth of "correct" costume should prove a mere excuse for arrested development.' 1999.

Georgian Lady – Kate Lister

ABOVE LEFT: Keen to enter the Costume Class at The Royal International Horse Show in 1997, Kate Lister settled for the 'painted, powdered, patched, perfumed' look of the Georgian lady. She rides her grey mare Summerville, bred by the famous Irish horsewoman, Iris Kellett.

'In 1748, so they say, and so I believe to be true, the King, walking in The Mall saw the Duchess of Bedford, riding in a blue riding-habit with white silk facings – this would be a man's skirted coat double breasted, a cravat,

a three-cornered-hat, and a full blue skirt. He admired her dress so much and thought it so neat that he straightaway ordered that the officers of the Navy, who, until now, had worn scarlet, should take this coat for the model of their new uniform. So did the Navy go into blue and white.' Dion Clayton Calthrop, English Costume *(A & C Black 1923).*

ABOVE RIGHT: Kate chose a red riding-habit – and surely would have caught the King's eye ... but here she is in more usual side-saddle dress. Hickstead 1996.

Circus

My Christmas holidays in London always included a visit to Bertram Mills' Circus at Olympia. I think the man who was fired from a cannon impressed me more than the horse acts, but, forty years on, I could marvel at the skill in riding three horses at once standing up. This is Austen Brothers' Circus.

The Field Marshal – Sir John Dill

From a tour bus at the National Cemetery at Arlington, Virginia, I caught sight of a large equestrian statue which looked unmistakably British. It was. Field Marshal Sir John Dill, the first non-American to be buried at Arlington, was head of the British Staff Mission in Washington 1941 – 1944. On his death, President Roosevelt sent a message to the Prime Minister: 'America joins with Great Britain in sorrow at the loss of your distinguished soldier, whose personal admirers here are legion'.

Winston Churchill thanked the President and, responding to General George C. Marshall and the United States Joint Chiefs of Staff said: 'He did all he could to make things go well, and they went well'. General Marshall later raised the money for the equestrian statue. I am happy that the final photograph in this book honours the memory of Sir John Dill, a British Field Marshal in the American Valhalla. 1988.

Acknowledgements

I wish to thank those whose support has led to the making of this book, notably all my subjects, for their patient understanding and readiness to face the ordeal of the camera.

I am especially grateful to the Crown Equerry, Lt. Colonel Seymour Gilbart-Denham, for permission to reproduce the photographs of the Royal Mews and ceremonial occasions taken in 1986. I was allowed special access to photograph by the then Crown Equerry, Lt. Colonel Sir John Miller, and I am most grateful to Sir John.

I must thank His Grace The Duke of Beaufort and his Joint Master, Captain Ian Farquhar for their help with my photography of the Beaufort Hunt – and my friends Gilbert and Pam Walshaw, who drove me the length and breadth of the country in pursuit of pictures.

I am further grateful to John Kendall and Freddie Monkhouse of Charles Kendall and Partners for their support.

There are others who helped me in checking the text including Lord Hugh Russell, Lady Clark, John Richards, Captain Brumwell, Adjutant The King's Troop, Royal Horse Artillery, Arthur Showell, Stephen Hadley, Allister Hood, Robert Bevis, Di Lampard, Richard Davison, Mary King, Kate Lister, Leslie Weller, David Braham, John Culverhouse and especially Penny Henderson, Secretary of Royal Windsor Horse Show, Elizabeth Inman, Secretary, and Julie Bishop of the Burghley Horse Trials Office, and Linda Reddy of The Royal Dublin Society.

On the technical side, I am grateful to Michael Connolly and Richard Nuttall of Michael Connolly Photography, Chester, my processing laboratory, and to Paul Cousins of Silverprint, London, for his advice and supply of darkroom materials.

I remember Alastair Simpson with grateful thanks. As founder of Airlife Books and Swan Hill Press he encouraged this book, but did not live to see it beyond the planning stage. His widow, Annabelle, and Publishing Director, Anne Walker, had the faith to go ahead. I thank them both and everyone at Swan Hill Press, particularly for the production skill of Rob Dixon and designer Glyn Griffin's refined eye for a picture on a page.

I am most grateful to my tireless assistant, Christine Evans, for coping with drafts, re-drafts, and for putting the text on disk. And, I thank my wife, Caroline, not only for her advice, but her patient forbearance as she saw her house engulfed by transparencies and other photographic trivia.

Lastly, I must mention three New York photographers ('… and if you can make it there, you can make it anywhere') Nancy Brown, Lucille Khornak and Uli Rose – your teaching provided the spur, and still does … thank you.

John Minoprio
Threapwood 2000